I GOT THIS!

The Making Of A Lion

Jamez Ingram

Printed in the United States of America

First printing December 2019

100 Fold Life Publishing

ISBN-13 - 978-1-7324084-3-2

Foreword

Have you ever desperately prayed to God for something or someone and wondered if He even heard you? Have you ever felt like your prayers are just hanging out in thin air, or that maybe God might have forgotten about you because the physical manifestation of the answer seems to be taking sooo loonngg?? And when you check back with God for the seventeenth time, His only answer to quench your longsuffering was, "I got this"?

God, I want my Dad to love me!

God, I need other men to follow!

God, I need a real friend!

God, I need a miracle!

God, I need a healing!

God, I need more strength!

God, I need faith!

God, I need to be taller!

God, I need more of you!

I Got This!

These are all the questions I asked God in my most troubling times and dire situations, and in His wonderful timing, these are just a few of the most life-changing requests He answered for me, but in a very different way than I expected.

Trust me, He hears you. He heard you the first time. Not only that, He already had the answer before you prayed it. God is a great listener. The greatest listener ever. He not only hears, He listens. He not only listens, He answers. Your prayers never return void. Just do your part and let God do His. He is always right on time, but you really have to trust his timing.

He got this.

I had to go on a journey, a trip into the unknown, to not only prepare myself for the life

He had planned for me, but also to stretch my faith and get rid of my limiting expectations. God told me who I was at an early age, and no matter what I went through or who let me down, God always showed up and had my back. When I would pray for His divine intervention into my life, His answer to me was always. *"I got this"*.

Love Eternally,
Wendy Ingram

Ps 145: "I will exalt you, my God the King; I will praise your name for ever and ever. Every day I will praise you and extol your name for ever and ever. Great is the LORD and most worthy of praise; his greatness no one can fathom. One generation commends your works to another; they tell of your mighty acts. They speak of the glorious splendor of your majesty—and I will meditate on your wonderful works"

Dedication

I would first like to dedicate this book to my Father in heaven for He has been with me every second of every day of my life starting in heaven up until today. I love you, Abba.

I would also like to thank my mother, Wendy Ingram, for everything that she has done for me every day of my life. She is not only the greatest mom a son could ever have, she's a warrior, a Queen, a prayer, a fighter, a teacher, and my greatest fan. I love you, Mom. Look what God had done for us! He got us

Contents

FOREWORD   III

DEDICATION   VI

THE PREQUEL   1

MAUI, HAWAII   13

BASKETBALL HEAVEN   21

ACCEPTING MY CALLING   29

GOD, ARE YOU STILL HERE?   37

CALIFORNIA BOUND   43

I HAD A DREAM   53

TIME FOR SURGERY   59

CAN YOU SAY ATTITUDE ADJUSTMENT?   67

PASSING MY TESTS   71

I AM WHO YOU SAY I AM   77

MY SENIOR YEAR   83

GOD'S WAYS ARE NOT OUR WAYS   91

I DO   101

GOD REALLY DOES SUPPLY ALL YOUR NEEDS   115

ADOPTION   125

LOVE LETTER TO JAMEZ   139

ABOUT THE AUTHOR...   **145**

1

The Prequel

Jos 1:9: "Have I not commanded you Be strong and courageous. Do not be afraid, do not be discouraged, for the Lord your God will be with you wherever you go"

I was born in 1986 to a teen mom and an absentee father who was distant and in and out of the picture most of my life. I was born on my exact due date, blue in color with the umbilical cord wrapped around my throat *twice*! But after 10 minutes of CPR, I took my first breath. I weighed 10 lbs. and was 23 inches long. According to my mom, she birthed a toddler.

My mom was young but very together. She didn't do drugs or drink alcohol. She was very excited to be a mom for 9 months. She read to me in her stomach and spoke to me about life, news and her views on life. She introduced me to hip-hop and a lot of other music and sang to me every day. She was bright, funny, and soon after I was born, found Jesus Christ as her lord and savior.

Throughout my life, she was not just my mom, she was the disciplinarian, my life coach, and spiritual compass. And after her many battles with cancer, strokes and Hashimoto's disease, she has become one of my heroes. She always focused on trying to raise me in a safe environment and being a good provider, which meant we had to move way too many times to count.

My mom was funny though. No matter where we moved, she always made sure that the first night in our new place was not only special, but that my room looked exactly the same as the last one. I am not sure how she was able to do that, but it always stuck with me and gave me peace. My mom loved learning and gave me a passion for writing and reading. I always had a thirst for knowledge for as long as I can remember. We traveled all over the United States. She taught me about culture and history, as well as music and food. In every state we visited, she made sure we visited museums and national landmarks. I loved drawing and creating as well as learning new and exciting things. Whether it was playing Legos or building things from my Erecto set, I just loved being busy and using my hands.

From an early age, I could remember my time in heaven before I was born. I loved learning about God growing up. All of my life, I've been labeled many things-from the doctors and teachers-like *genius, creative, unusual, gifted,* and from my pastors I was always being referred to as an "*old soul.*" I've always cared about animals, homeless people, and others who were hurting. My empathetic giftings and my thirst for God allowed me to use my gifts of healing and discernment at a very young age. I attribute most of that to my mom because she studied the word thoroughly and prayed for God's wisdom on how to encourage my gifts rather than be afraid of them.

I was full of love and life. My mother said, "*I was not just a happy baby, but a joyful baby always giggling and chatting with people and asking a million and one questions.*" This made me different in a good way. I always sat with the adults at church and listened to the pastors. I didn't like the nursery, I wanted to know big things, important things. I still do.

Once I was school age, I was tested and they said I had a very high IQ. That combined with a photogenic memory and a strong spiritual connection with God made me different. I was blessed to meet and be prophesied over by a lot of well-known men of God, like Tommy Barnett, Benny Hinn, Jack Hayford, James Morocco. I received the gift of tongues by age 4. But even though these mighty men spoke powerful words into my life, the man I wanted to speak into my life, wouldn't. That man was my biological father with whom I desperately desired to have a relationship with.

I was an only child, well, sort of. I had a brother, but only for a few days. I was only two so I don't have any memory of him. His name was Caleb. So even though I was raised as an only child, I really wasn't. But thank God I had amazing grandparents and great-grandparents with whom I was able to spend a lot of time with in my early years.

Oh yeah, I did have a dog named Holly. My mom got her for me when I was 10 years-old. My counselor had told my mom it would help me with moving so much since I was an only child. We went to the pound to pick out a dog and she broke free off her leash and ran right into my arms. She was on her way to be put down but I saved her. And she very much saved me over the years. She was my very best friend and knew all of my secrets and dreams. She was a great listener, too. She lived till my 23rd birthday, so in dog years, she was quite old. I still shed a tear when I think about her or look at her picture hanging on my office wall.

Another constant in my life, besides Jesus and my mom, was sports. Sports helped me to fit in no matter where we moved to. I loved soccer, skateboarding and basketball. But as I grew older and taller, basketball became my passion. Since my dad was a coach, I thought it would help me connect to him in some weird way, but it didn't. It actually pushed him further away.

Because of sports, I never had trouble talking to kids, not even at school. I wanted friends and I even tried to keep in touch with them when I moved. I sure wish Facebook was around back then. I would've definitely kept in touch with a lot of my friends at school. But my teachers, hmm not so much. I was a good student. I never really caused any teacher any problems, but for some reason, many of my teachers did not like me, especially when I talked about Jesus. One teacher in particular was a junior high teacher of mine. She tried over and over again to get me to take off my "true love waits" purity ring. I was not brought up religious and judgmental. Instead, due to my giftings of empathy and healing, I just loved God and I had a personal relationship with Him so I talked about Him like others talked about their family and friends.

Regardless of my efforts to explain this to her, she would send me to the principal's office for no reason other than I was being insubordinate. I was different and so I was an easy target for bullies. I loved Jesus and I had "big ears," so the bullies would say. These differences made me a target for those boys who would see me on the court. and try to pick me apart. I didn't always understand that at the time, but of course, as an adult hindsight is always 20/20. To this day, I thank those bullies. They made me work harder and smarter on and off the court. My heart was just to connect with other boys, usually hoping to find older boys that could be a mentor for me and fill that void I had of an absent father.

So, for the most part I was probably a pretty "normal" kid (so I thought). Though I've endured divorced parents, various forms of bullying—from being sexually assaulted, incurring a broken shoulder, and being called names day after day—I would still call my childhood pretty normal. Thank God I was really good in sports for these became my go-to for outlets. School was easy. I got good grades, especially in reading and writing. I had a little difficulty with math until I understood math was money, then boom, I got it!

Since my teachers had labeled me a genius, I had an individualized tutor. That's how the school dealt with extremely smart students. They either promoted us a grade higher or gave us individualized tutoring because normal schoolwork bored the heck out of us. I chose the latter. I had this one reading tutor who as a godsend to a young boy looking for a father figure for affirmation, even though he didn't know God. But I was someone who longed to not only fit in, but I crave a father to teach me how to be a "*man*". That is a void a mom, no matter how great, can never fill. But my reading tutor did.

Don't get me wrong, my mom taught me great values, how to make and save money, how to handle conflict, how to pray and ask God for guidance, how to treat a woman, and take care of myself and a household. She even helped me learn how to camp and love the outdoors and how to work on cars. But I was hungry for more.

I wanted and needed a warrior, a man who feared God and fought battles on their knees.

I tried reaching out to my youth pastors and coaches, but they never seemed to be as in-tune to God as I was. Plus, I had met so many incredible pastors early on in my life that I wanted, craved and desired to be challenged in new ways. I would just spend hours reading my word and trying to figure out how to be not just a "man," but a "*godly man*" that would live a life for God, a warrior in His mighty army. I knew I was supposed to be a leader and a teacher, and maybe even a pastor, but how could I become any of those things if I didn't have any men show me how. So, I decided to study the men of the bible.

I did this all the way through my junior high years and into high school. Once in high school, I made the varsity basketball team, I joined a youth group at my church that I was really connected to. I was in heaven. I was being mentored by very upstanding adults, I was on the varsity basketball team, and I had friends. And then one night, I came home to, "*What do you think about moving to Maui?* My father, who was recently back in the picture, was offered a job there. My mom would be able to retire from her job and do full-time ministry, but they said I had the final say. *Really?* I didn't even know what Maui, Hawaii was but I was not going to be the one to say no. So, I prayed about it and God's answer was, "I got this." So, I told them '*Yes*'. Two weeks later, we moved to Hawaii.

From that day on, my life was forever changed.

2

Maui, Hawaii

*Rom 8:28: "And we know that in all things God
works for the good of those who love him... What
then , shall we say in response to these things? If
God is for us, who can be against us?"*

We arrived early in the morning. It was 90
degrees or at least it felt like was. It was the
beginning of summer vacation and my new life.
This place was so different. As we drove down
the two-lane roads, the landscape was just out of
some type of fairytale; the bluest sky and water

I'd ever seen, sprouting palm trees, crystal clear pools and lush green parks as far as I could see. Once we settled into our hotel, we immediately began to explore this wondrous land. The ocean was so clear and the water was so warm. I decided right away I was going to make the best of this. We had not been on a vacation in a few years and I just wanted time with my mom and dad. But secretly, I was hoping this change in atmosphere would help my father finally settle down and want to be a father to me. I was still hopeful he would receive Jesus into his heart, love my mom and me, and we'd start fresh and become a real family again. Boat trips, water-parasailing, snorkeling, and mastering the boogie board and then the surfboard became my new norm.

My mom found us a church right away and we were off. I joined the youth group and my mom seemed to be the happiest I had ever seen her. The pastor, Dr. James Morocco, was like Moses, a large man with a powerful voice but such a gentle way about him. He didn't just preach the word of God, he taught it. I could tell he knew Jesus and that he was the man that would finally answer all of my questions. He was an answer to a lot of my prayers from earlier in life.

Right away, I signed up for every class that Dr. Morocco was teaching. He is a historian and a storyteller who can dive you so deep into the word that you are transported back in time. My mom joined the choir and drama team and I began to meet a lot of great youth, including my youth leaders. They saw me. They saw that I had a call on life. They invited me to speak and asked me to help put on youth events. They called me a youth leader. Hmm, I started thinking to myself, maybe this move really was for me.

I dived into this church full steam ahead. I studied my bible night and day, and when I learned they had a high school, I asked my mom if I could attend it. Once she looked into it, she said, Yes". Yes! I immediately felt like I was home. This is a place where I could gain wisdom and insight. I would finally be around men who loved God and could teach me what I needed to know.

Becoming a Hawaiian was not as easy. Assimilating into different cultures had never been a problem for me. I have always loved all people. In California, I was mixed but my color was never talked about. But here, I was the minority, they called me *"howlie"*, which means breath or ghost. A lot of my friends had parents that were in ministry so they were not looking for God or didn't even want to serve God. But the teachers were all spirit filled and so knowledgeable about not just the history of God, but of His living power, I just soaked it all in.

I wanted to be liked by the kids, too, so I did what I do and tried out for the basketball team… and made it! Varsity basketball, 24-hour chapel, and no judgment for my faith, I had hit the lottery!

I grew by leaps in bounds. No more having to debate with others in my youth group about speaking in tongues. I was with youth that earnestly cried out for a move of God like I wanted. Youth group became such an extension of family, I recruited my mom to come and speak to them.

Her revelation of the Holy Spirit radically changed our whole groups way of worshipping and praying. Miracles started happening and we were all kids in our service. We had a great youth pastor who really loved God and had a real passion for seeing youth grow, not just play activities and babysitting us. He too taught us and allowed us to participate fully in the services. Our youth group had its own band, sound crew, and outreach team. We were even holding bible studies on local high school campuses. This was so different from my past. I finally had people that wanted to see Jesus move in powerful ways. We wanted to see people get healed. We wanted to see God move in signs and wonders. Every service we would be up at the front worshipping and crying out to God. Every service.

Because of all of the worshipping and praying I did, the pain of not having a father--and being bullied by other kids and teachers for my faith-- was becoming a distant memory. God healed my heart and brought other men in my life that were encouraging me and helping me to understand who I was in God. I was on top of the world.

Hallelujah!

3

Basketball Heaven

Jer 29:11-13: "For I know the plans I have for you,
` declares the Lord, "plans to prosper you and not
to harm you, plans to give you hope and a future.
Then you will call on me and come and pray to
me, and I will listen to you. You will seek me and
find me when you seek me with all your heart."

I had a great basketball coach named Curtis
Jackson. He was not only a talented ball player; *he*
was a preacher! He taught me how to be a *"dulos"*
athlete, how to press in for greatness even when

super-talented, and how to be a good sport and have a good attitude on and off the court.

I traveled to every island and played my heart out for him. I just knew God was telling me I would go pro and use my talent to lead others to Jesus. I would talk to the other players about Jesus and about the things that God was showing me. But most of them were not as passionate about him as I was. One night I was talking to my mom about my visions and dreams of traveling and playing pro ball and leading kids to Christ. She was trying to encourage me but kept saying what a bad life the NBA is and that my call was bigger as a pastor. That was frustrating to say the least. I wanted to serve God, but being a pastor in a church did not seem to fit me. Don't get me wrong, I loved sharing my faith with others, but I saw myself as sharing my testimonies with non-believers and encouraging them that God loved them. That's what was appealing to me. Loving the unlovable like my mom did when she was an evangelist, not doing the paper work and day to day church operations like she was doing now.

My heart was for homeless people, the unlovable, the gang members and the people others had written off. I had always loved going to soup kitchens, feeding the homeless and giving them shoes and clothes and hearing their stories of how they ended up there. I spent many Easter breaks going to other countries to build homes and even churches for the less fortunate, this is what inspired me. I just went to my room and got on my knees, and began crying out to God, *"Speak to me. Tell me what you made me for. Whatever you want, my life belongs to you."*

Then it happened. We had been given a flyer at chapel; a guest speaker was coming to our church. The flyer read:

"Damon Thompson travels to various churches, conferences, and gatherings, releasing the spirit of awakening through a prophetic call to renewed hunger for God. He wants to see believers equipped to fulfill their current, immediate destiny of carrying revival. He desires to be a sword in the hands of local ministries to effectively establish the Kingdom of God in people's lives. He also longs to see true spiritual fathers raised up that will develop mature sons to become voices of awakening."

I knew I had to meet him. He was not just an evangelist who spoke on the heart of God and loving the unlovely, he was stirring up the atmosphere and awakening my soul. I was in a sea of people--there was over 1000 people there, yet, I felt like he came just to talk to me. I came with a notebook and my bible ready and willing. He spoke on starting a fire and being the fire of God, moving in signs and wonders. He held nothing back. I read books on Smiths Wigglesworth and other evangelist who were bold in Christ, Damon had that same spark. I knew in the pit of my stomach that I needed to have that, too. I wanted everything God said in His word was for me. I wanted to encounter God in this way, where I would see His glory and help set people free.

Then all of a sudden, in the middle of speaking, he stops and says, "The Lord has a word for somebody." My head was down because I had been taking massive quantities of notes. He begins describing the person, and then I felt a nudge. My mom says to me, "I think he's looking at you." So I looked up and he was staring right into my eyes and said, "You son, yes you, come up here." My heart was pounding and my knees were shaking as I got out of me seat and headed up the aisle. As I was walking up, he told everyone to pray in the spirit, that God was here and the Holy Spirit is moving in this place. By the time I got on stage, Damon was speaking in tongues and crying out to God for a fresh fire. Then my eyes met his and he spoke not just to me, but to my soul. I felt my spirit rise up, like I was ten feet tall.

He said, "Son, God sees you and he has destined you to greatness. He has put his heart inside you. You may be a kid in the natural, but you son are a giant among men. God has given you much wisdom, way beyond your years, and He has called you to start fires and go into the dark places and set the captives free!" Then he put his hand on my stomach and said, "I transfer my mantel to you. I pray my ceiling is your floor." My legs and whole body gave way and I fell back in the spirit. Next thing I remember is being in the heavens, seeing lights that were so bright and feeling tingling all over my whole body. When I woke, I was being walked off the stage by my youth pastor and friend.

My mom threw her arms around my neck and whispered through her tears, "I told you you were special, set apart for Him," she whispered. I had no idea what this meant at the time, but I knew I really wanted all God had for me. So, I started an outreach with my youth pastor at the church's gym, a way for young men to come and play pick-up basketball games *and* be fed the word of God.

I was so very very happy. My life was finally having some sense of direction and purpose. I even told God if you need me to give up basketball, I will gladly. Over the next several months, I was just soaking in the word, going to the chapel playing basketball, and loving my new life.

4

Accepting My Calling

Ps 46:10 (NIV): "He says, "Be still and know that I am God; I will be exalted among the nations, I will be exalted in the earth."

One afternoon, my mom came in my room after being away at a women's event and said she needed to repent to me for saying that God wouldn't want me to play pro basketball, and that she was very sorry to steal any dream given to me by God.

She asked for my forgiveness and I accepted it, but in the back of my mind, I was thinking, "Okay God, I guess we are doing it all. So as she left me room, I thought it is on now! I fell to my knees and said, "God, I am all yours. Use me for your glory." That was the day I accepted my call and things became clearer than ever before. I knew I needed to be equipped so I asked my mom if I could attend seminary over the summer, and of course she said, "Yes."

Our church had a seminary school at a remote location up in HYKU. It had bunk beds, a wood stove, and cold showers, but I didn't care. I wanted to discover who I was and my purpose. We helped the pastors and attended services all week long at our many locations. We did outreaches and we learned how to serve God in many different ways.

Every morning, I woke up so happy knowing who I was and who God intended for me to be. I trained harder, studied more and was giving everything 100 percent. I even started praying and fasting more for my father and his eternal life.

I felt so close to God, my praise became purposeful and I wanted to have excellence in every area of my life so that God would know how much I loved him.

To top off that season, our varsity basketball team made it to the playoffs. Right before our first game, I am in the locker room and as the chaplain is praying over us, I hear God say, "Trust me, I got this". I just smiled and said, "Amen." Excited for the game, I just knew we were destined to win the championship. We were playing against a private school, Seabury Hill. I was only a sophomore, but I was hungry to get a championship to try to impress my father.

In the second quarter, I leaped in the air and grabbed a rebound, and as I headed down the court, I looked to my left, then my right, there was no one in sight. So I drove it down it down the middle of the lane for a layup. As I leaped again, a guard from the other team clipped my leg and I plummeted to the ground -- SSMMAACKK!! I tried to jump up quickly as if it didn't hurt, but the pain in my leg was *excruciating*! Come to find out my leg was out of the socket. First my coach, then the school's nurse, then my parents rushed onto the court. They carried me off the court and the next thing I know, I am going to the hospital by ambulance. "But it's only the second quarter!," I yelled. As the ambulance sped down the city streets with sirens blaring, needles and IVs were being put into my arm. Suddenly, my head started swirling as I dozed off. I saw Jesus. He showed me that He was with me and that I was going to be ok. I heard Him say, "I got this."

I woke up to people rushing around, doctors ordering tests, and nurses running in and out of my room. It seemed like an eternity before the ER doctors said to me, "I think it just came out the socket, but let's do an Xray to be sure". Hours later, the pain medication begins wearing off and I kept saying," I just want to go back to the game".

Then an eerie feeling overcame the room as the doctors reentered. What they said to me and my family next changed my life in a split-second. The doctors said, "There's a tumor growing out of your bone." I heard nothing else he said. I just kept quiet. I kept waiting for God to say, "I got this." But instead, I had deafening silence. *"God, where are you? I need you right now?"* Tears began to roll down my face. My mom kept saying, "God's got you, you're going to be ok." The doctors left my side but were still talking on the other side of the curtain trying to determine what to do for me now. Then my mom joined them and went into medical detective mode. She asked questions, gathered phone numbers of specialists, asked for copies of the tests and Xrays—that's my mom. I looked over to see my father sitting there toatally checked out, looking down at his phone getting the latest sports scores. *Really??!*

Later that night, the Lord woke me up and gave me these scriptures;

Is 41:10: "Do not fear, for I am your God. I will strengthen you and help you; I will uphold you with my righteous right hand."

1 Ptr 5:7: "Cast all your anxiety on him because he cares for you."

Ps 55:22: "Cast your cares on the Lord and he will sustain you; he will never let the righteous be shaken."

Tears streamed down my face as I lay in bed wrapped in ace bandages that were trying to hold my leg together. I felt like a mummy. I was afraid to make any sudden moves that would cause me any more pain than I already had. I laid there in bed staring at the crutches in the corner of the room thinking, "How did I get here?" How come this is happening to me?" God, I don't understand? You said, "You got this." What do you got? I'm in pain and I can not walk!"

5

God, Are You Still Here?

Deut 31:6: "Be strong and courageous. Do not be afraid or terrified because of them, for the Lord your God goes with you; he will never leave you nor forsake you"

As the pain medication wore off, the excruciating pain came back with a vengeance. My leg and my groin felt like it was on fire. All I could do is yell for my mom. I was so independent before, so to constantly ask my mom to help me even to sit up, roll over, or use the bathroom was humiliating. My mom came running in, and as usual, was more than happy to help with a tray of food, some medication and a great big smile. The calm in her face was my faith. I know she knew what it was like to be in pain, to be ill, to fight battles, so her lack of fear was my only resource of faith and keeping my peace

Maui does not have any specialist doctors or main hospitals that are equipped to handle this kind of thing. So, they told my parents that I had to fly to Oahu to be seen by specialists. Trying to figure out how to get me in a car and on a plane was another hurtle to overcome. But my mom made calls and finalized all of the pertinent details. All I could do was be still. Very still. Meanwhile, I was doing everything I could to hear from God: listening to worship music, reading and studying my bible and getting prayer from my church. These were the only things I cared about for the next several weeks while I waited to get all the tests I needed approved so I could go get them done and then get a plan in place! My mind wondered to weird places. Questions I never thought I would have to contemplate danced through my head; what if they have to amputate my leg, would I wear a fake one. Could I still become a one-legged pro basketball player? Maybe I can play in a wheelchair league. Do they have a pro basketball wheelchair league? My mind was racing.

On crutches and not really able to walk or do much, I just stayed in my room trying desperately to hear from God. I started to doubt that I had been hearing from God all these months. I started to question myself, my beliefs and my heart. I just could not erase all those confirmations I had gotten. The only person I talk to about everything I was feeling was my mom. She had overcome every battle of sickness ever thrown at her. She must have all my answers. My mom was a rock. She answered my health questions and gave me the scriptures she stood on. She explained that in every battle she had gone through, it was for a deeper purpose and I needed to keep trusting God. My mom is a warrior at heart, but I could see that she too was shook up. All of us were going to be tested through this.

All the pastors began calling and checking on us daily. I have to say for being part of a "megachurch", it was amazing that Dr. Morocco knew us by name. He called me and he prayed for me and always ended our conversations by saying 'keep him updated.' Four weeks later, yes, an entire month later, we were finally getting a call The doctor on Oahu said that I would have to have my leg cut at the groin, have the leg bone taken out, *and then* saw out part of my femur neck to get rid of the tumor and insure that there were no pieces left. *But* they could not make any guarantees because a) they would not know until after they took it out if it was cancer and what kind and b) if this procedure is done, they couldn't be for certain if I would be able to ever walk again because they would have to graft the bone and insert three pins and a rod to hold it in place, and c) that I would become sterile due to the cutting into the groin where it was attached to . Okay, let's stop right here and let that sink in. I'm 14 years-old and the doctor's telling me that not only I may never walk again! *And* no one has said anything at all about cancer to us before right now. And what the hell does being sterile mean??

I told my doctor that's not an option for me. I will just believe God for my healing. The surgeon was shocked and said, Well, at least let me send him to UCLA in California and see what the specialist there thinks." My mom nodded and the nurse got on the phone and gave her the appropriate phone numbers and other pertinent information.

My mom looked at me with those happy, but fearful eyes and said it's my decision. She's saying that in her head, but I know her heart was hurting. So, I told her I would at least go and listen. So, the wait began again, first to get travel arrangements together and then the endless calls to get all the approvals from the insurance company.

6

California Bound

Ps 91: (NIV)1: *"Whoever dwells in the shelter of the Most High, will rest in the shadow of the Almighty*

It was so unbearably painful to get around. My hip and my leg were still bound with reams of bandages and I was still on crutches. But worst of all, I felt shooting pains throughout my entire body, especially in my groin and inner thigh, day and night. It would wake me up all hours of the night. I hated it. I felt like I had no control over anything in body, let alone my life. I did my best to hide how I was truly feeling from everyone, especially my mom. She had enough to worry about; I didn't want to add this to her plate. I even hid it from my father because I didn't want to hear his go-to advice and wisdom in matters like these, which was "Suck it up. Stop being a baby." I was used to being the healer, the encourager, the motivator, but this type of situation was uncharted territory for me. I finally had to admit to myself that I didn't know how to navigate this. As I tried to wrap my mind around what was happening to me, I started remembering times during basketball practice when I couldn't complete defensive slides after a sharp, paralyzing pain in my groin would be so excruciating, it would take my breath away. Then the next questions flooded in: *When did it start?*

How did it start? How long has it been there? Did I cause it? What caused it? These questions consumed every second of my attention on the plane ride to California. As soon as I landed, I felt my spirit perk up and I also heard got say I got this.

Now California was home to me--I was born there and lived there until we moved to Maui--so going home felt like just what I needed. My mom made all of the necessary appointments with the doctors and she also organized meetups with my cousins and my old friends from school and church so that I could keep busy and not think about all this stuff.

The next day, we arose early and headed to UCLA Hospital. It is an enormous, world-renowned teaching hospital. There are herds of doctors and nurses going every which way quickly. We got into the biggest elevator I had ever seen in my life. It was a big as my bedroom.

As the elevator started to climb, I started envisioning the doctor. How he would look? Would he look like all of those doctors on tv: tall, handsome, and drove a fancy car or was he one of the weird, crazy looking doctors in a horror movie? One cool thing I had heard about this doctor was he treated NBA player. I wanted to play in the NBA, he treated NBA players, my hope began to rise.

My hope continued to percolate as we sat in his office. AS he was speaking, all I could hear him say was NBA this, NBA that. But as continued, I noticed the demeanor on his face started to change. Then I finally tuned into what he was saying to us. "Yes, I can do this surgery, and I can even cut you open from the posterior and pull out the femur to get to the femoral neck bone, however, you will never play ball again and you will most likely not walk or walk with a cane, and fertility could be an issue later. "Not again," I exclaimed as my little bitty hope was crushed into a million pieces. He went onto say, "And furthermore, it would be two separate procedures." The first procedure would be to cut that piece of the femur out and put in a rod, screws, and bone graft. Then after that healed and set, a second surgery would be done to go in and remove the screws and rod. *Nope!*, that was not going to work for me. The doctor could tell I was not having it, so he just looked at me and my mom and said, "He is a young man, not a kid, and he needs to be settled in his spirit that he wants this or he won't fight hard to come back from it. So, give him time to figure out what he is willing to go through. Whatever your decision is, I will be here." Then he shook our hands and we left. Back in that massive elevator, my heart sank and my hope dissipated. My dreams started to look like fading wishes. My mom just looked at me and said, "Just breathe; we don't have to figure this out today. God's got this".

On the plane ride back to Hawaii, I began to pray and ask God to give me a plan, or a sign that he wanted me to have this surgery. I leaned my head back on the seat rest on the plane and whispered this scripture,

Prv 3:5-6: "Trust in the Lord with all your heart and lean not on your own understanding; In all your ways submit to him; and he will make your paths straight."

Okay God, I give this to you. Show me my path.'

Waiting on God is never as easy as you think, especially when there is an enormous clock ticking in your ear. All day long, the doctor's words swirled in my head. The scriptures were telling me to *rest, keep my peace* and to *trust God.* My heart believed God and all His word says about me, but my mind was trying to bring fear by thinking of all the what ifs? Cancer is painful. My hip and leg were in a looot of pain, and thinking that pain could get a 100x worse or that if I waited too long to make up my mind, I could possibly die, that's a lot to consider for anyone, let alone a 14-year-old. Have the surgery and never play ball again or have kids or don't have the surgery and then I won't be around to be a · father anyway. Wow, this cannot be my only option.

The more time that passed, the more my woe is me attitude started to infiltrate my mind. The more I thought about what was happening to me, the angrier I started to get, mainly at myself for allowing fear to have any place in my mind. I kept asking God, "Why do I need to go through this at all?! Why?" Then my mom came into my room and said, "Here is my watch; you get 5 more minutes to feel sorry for yourself and then you are done. When your 5 minutes are up, meet me in the living room." Like I said before, my mom is a cancer survivor, so quitting is not an option. So, I woed for 5 minutes, then grabbed my notebook and bible and met her in the living room.

We made a list of all my promises from God and all the questions that I could ever possibly think of and then we answered as many as we could, and then went to our bible for the rest. My confidence started to come back. A few hours had gone by and my mom said, "Okay, we did our part; now we let God do His." *This is how you grow your faith,* by trusting in what you cannot see. But God!...

As we prayed, we asked God and the Holy Spirit to give me a dream or vision so that I would know exactly what to do. That why I love The Holy Spirit so much. He is our comforter and teacher in all things. He is the only one who can tell you the truth about your future. The only one. But He's a gentleman. He waits to be asked, so we asked.

Prv 3:5-6'Trust in the Lord with all your heart and lean not on your own understanding; In all your ways submit to him; and he will make your paths straight".

Afterwards, we ate dinner, watched a funny movie, and then I went to sleep. It still had not really hit me, I was still not at full peace, but I was focused on God and His Word.

Jn 14:15-17 (NIV): "If you love me, keep my commands. And I will ask the Father, and he will give you another advocate(comforter) to help you and be with you forever—the Spirit of truth. The world cannot accept him, because it neither sees him nor knows him. But you know him, for he lives with you and will be in you.

7

I Had A Dream

*Is 53:5: "But He was wounded for our
transgressions, He was bruised for our iniquities;
The chastisement for our peace was upon him,
and by His stripes we are healed."*

I prayed every day. I knew God would answer
my question in His timing, so I asked my mom
could I go back to school until He told me what
to do. She said okay. Meanwhile, the pain in my
groan was getting worse. Frustration tried to
creep in. Reality was really starting to set in, "Oh

God!, I have CANCER and I am ONLY 14!

God, you still got this, right?

God knew I could not do this alone so He surrounded me with a lot of mighty men of God, like my basketball coach, Curtis Jackson, who frequently came by to encourage me and help me to see that God would use all this for his glory and that this was God's opportunity to show up and do something miraculous.

About a week after we got back from California, I had a dream. The dream was very real, and it stuck. I was back in time and I saw Jesus on the cross. Then I walked up a hill and Jesus was sitting on a rock. He stuck out his hands and showed me the scars in his hands and feet. Then I walked a little further towards a big door and when I opened it, I was now at the hospital. I got on the operating table and started to speak to the team of doctors. *I told them* that they were going to cut me and *gently* pull the leg out and the tumor will then fall off on its own. When that happens, then you just put my leg back in, sew me up, and God will do the rest.

I quickly woke up and started writing all of it down so that I could share it with my parents in the morning. As I started to write the words, it hit me, *cut my leg??* All kinds of thoughts started racing through my head, so I got up and put on my worship music to drown it all out. I refused to start living in fear; I started to give myself a pep talk. During breakfast I showed my mom what I had written down and she said she had a similar dream, and that everyone in the waiting room gave their hearts to Jesus as soon as the doctor told us the good news.

My mom had suggested earlier that week to make an appointment with Dr. Marocco, our pastor. That day, he called to say he was available

later that afternoon, so we went to see him. As I
said earlier, Dr. Marocco is a great pastor and has
so much wisdom that you feel blessed to even get
five minutes with him. That day, he talked to me
for several hours as my mom waited in the lobby.
He started telling me about all of the different
ways God answer prayers and that I needed to be
open to any and all of His ways. Then I shared
my dream with him. Before I could finish telling
him, tears started flowing down his cheek. I
couldn't understand why, was my dream that
crazy? He wiped his face with his handkerchief
and said he, too, had, had a very similar dream
the night before which is why he wanted to meet
with me today. He prayed with me and I felt the
Holy Spirit come and put His arm around me. I
never felt God like this before. I had so much
peace. God is so faithful. I was so happy that He
did not just give the dream to me, He also game

me two people who would support me and pray in agreement with me.

Mt 18:20: "For where two or three gather in my name, there am I with them."

8

Time For Surgery

Mind you, I still wanted a miracle, and I was not going to focus on fear, but faith. So, I began looking up scriptures that would tell my family how I felt and how to be in agreement for my miracle. I began to talk to God and ask him what scriptures to use. Then I wrote a letter to them that included the sinner's prayer at the end. After I typed it all up, my mom took it and had copies made, which she handed out to everyone the day of the surgery in the waiting room. Here's the letter:

Dear family and friends,

Today, I am agreeing to have this surgery, but I am believing God for a miracle. I believe God will take the tumor off without them having to drill my bone, or insert screws or a plate and rod in my leg. I am also believing that if it is a Cancer, that God will heal me, without any chemotherapy. I trust God. I am saved and I know God will be by my side. If any of you doubt God, please don't feel free to stay. I need people to walk in agreement and cannot have any negative talk. I am also believing that God will use this for his glory, so if you don't yet know Jesus as your personal savior, please feel free to say the pray below that would be the biggest gift to give me.

"Father, I know that my sins have separated me from you. I am truly sorry, and now I want to repent for my past sins. Please forgive me. I now believe that your son, Jesus Christ, died on the cross for my sins, was resurrected, and is alive. Today, I invite Jesus Christ to be my Lord and my Savior from this day forward. Please send your Holy Spirit to dwell within me for the rest of my life. In Jesus' name I pray, Amen."

Love James

I believed with my mom for healings before but that was different; now I am actually going to have to be put under anesthesia and be cut. I trust God, but I was afraid of the doctor making a mistake or him not really doing what I asked. So, I decided to pray for the doctors. This helped me feel so much more peaceful. Again, I heard that soft, calming voice say, "I got this."

On the way to California, we were notified that my great-grandfather on my father's side was having open heart surgery, so I made a stop to see him before checking into my hospital. I always had a special bond with him. My father and grandfather were not connected to me like he was. I could talk to him about God, basketball and life things. He was a great man who did a lot for his family and I always looked to him for wisdom. He knew, which is why he requested to see me before his surgery, that he would not be able to be with me. He wanted me to be tough for him and he was going to be tough for me during his surgery. He was 85 so his was surgery was very risky. I knew my great-grandpa had faith and was walking with God so I was able to have peace about his surgery while gaining the confidence to go through with mine.

Both my parents and most of my grandparents came to the hospital, even some aunts and uncles and cousins and friends came out to show their support. After the IV was inserted, they started the medicine, which just made me relax. It's really hard to prepare for the unknown, but I can say this, my doctor and his team were super-confident. They each came in and shook my hand firmly. We went over the "game plan", as he called it. He kept saying. "I got this. I guarantee you I will do my best to follow all your requests, but remember, I am only doing the surgery, the miracle is on God." This made me smile ear to ear--probably because the medicine was kicking in. I just looked to my parents, gave a thumbs up, and then went to sleep.

Hours later, I awoke to three nurses shaking my arm, talking to me, and letting me know I was all done. I was woozy and thinking how can that be? I just dozed off for what seemed like a few minutes. The pain was way more than I ever imagined. The pain medicine was having an allergic reaction as I was trying to fight back tears of pain. I actually thought I would come out all healed and pain free--you really can't understand the process if you have never gone through it.

I kept yelling at the nurses, "Please find my mom."

Finally, she was able to see me. She had a huge smile on her face and told me, "It happened just like your dream! It popped off, no pins, yeah!" My response? "Who cares? This pain is unreal" Not my finest moment, but thank you God for grace.

As she noticed how much pain I was in, her smile turned upside down. She started asking me questions, checking the pain medication, and then went to get the nurse. It seems I was having a huge allergic reaction to the pain medication. Once it was changed, all of my fears left and I apologized to my mom for screaming at her earlier. She understood and forgot about it.

My father on the other hand stayed only for a few minutes and then left. It was hard for him to see me like that. He tried to comfort me, but again, his thing is just 'suck it up'. Um, no that doesn't help me. My leg is hanging in the air, I've got a catheter and staples running down my hip, and it feels like I have to pee all the time. It felt like my leg was literally ripped out of me. But thank God, after only a couple of days in the hospital, I was able to leave. I started to get my peace of mind back, finally, taking it one day at a time.

9

Can You Say Attitude Adjustment?

You think you know how you will act in a situation until that situation becomes your new reality. Pain, Fear, Frustration, Fatigue and Free Will all come into play when you undergo an intense surgery where the main muscles, secondary muscles, nerves and bone have been cut, exposed and manipulated. Your body is angry and has an opinion about everything. I had to learn the mental recovery before the physical recovery would come into alignment.

I went to stay with my mom's father, my grandma Melinda, and my parents as the road to recovery began. I had a home health nurse and a physical therapist to help me get around and work with me on mind over matter. I literally had to go to the bathroom in a new way, use crutches everywhere I went, drag along a numb leg that didn't want to move. Discouragement came and attacked me like a thief in the night--and my attitude was not helping. I had no grace for myself. Everyone understood this was a process but me. I'm used to taking out my frustrations on the court, or on my skateboard, but not now. I took it out on the people around me. *Come on leg, work!,* then nothing. You don't realize how much stuff your legs do in a day without even thinking about it. But when you have to think of every task and how you're going to execute it, you grow an appreciation for that body part, quickly. By the time you're done with one task, it's nap time. No more Supermaaan!, just James.

The best thing that happened to me during this time was my grandfather. He brought home a computer in pieces with a blueprint and said, "Here, stop thinking and put this together for me." Building that computer forced me to give myself a break. It also helped build my confidence that there is still plenty of things I can do. It made me snap out of my pity-party and go into my Word. I cried out to the Holy Spirit for comfort and wisdom. He taught me how to retrain my mind to make my leg follow. It was amazing.

Phi 4:13: "I can do all things through Christ Jesus who strengthens me."

Jesus would show up many a night to remind me of our plans and the stripes he took on the cross for me.

Phi 4:19: "And my God shall supply all your need according to His riches in glory by Christ Jesus.

After the staples came out, I could finally go back to Maui, back to my home, back to my refuge, back to my life.

Prv 3:5-6 (KJV)
"Trust in the Lord with all thine heart; and lean not unto thine own understanding.
In all thy ways acknowledge him, and he shall direct thy paths.

10

Passing My Tests

Jam 1:2-4 (ESV): "Count it all joy, my brothers, when you meet trials of various kinds, for you know that the testing of your faith produces steadfastness. And let steadfastness have its full effect, that you may be perfect and complete, lacking in nothing."

You don't realize it when you give your life to God that you will be tested. Oh, but you will, and I was and still am. As you grow in God, there is a real enemy trying to fill you with fear and doubt, and make you think this whole God thing may not be real. It's up to you to pray, study your Word daily, talk to God daily, seek council from the Holy Spirit daily, and then, trust the process. The best way to strengthen yourself under trials and tests is to fill yourself up with God and pour yourself out to Him with praise and thanksgiving.

I was so grateful to be spending my summer in seminary, which is just a fancy way of saying bible camp. It's not really 'roughing it' when it's a cabin in the lush forests of Maui. But with all I had just gone through, I was just hungry for more of God. He showed up and was faithful in my time of need. He did exactly what He said He would, even if it didn't look exactly like the picture in my head. God did do it, and He was still doing it daily. My heart was so full of gratitude that I couldn't wait for another encounter with God. Me and seven other young men up in a cabin, roughing it, ready to deny my flesh and press in for more of God. Reading my Word has always been a comfort to me, but I read all of its stories as if they were history lessons. Now I am discovering that this Word is the breath of God, living for us *today*! It is full of promises, wisdom, comfort and hidden treasures just for me. I was quickly learning that I need God on this journey called life.

Right before I left for 'seminary', my bags all packed, my favorite snacks ready to go, the doctor from California who did my surgery called with news that stopped me in my tracks. He informed my parents and I that the tumor wasn't just a tumor, it was in fact a type of bone cancer, and that he felt he got it all out. I asked him did he think I needed to do chemo and he asked me, "What does God say?" I said, "I don't know, but I will ask." We laughed and I thanked him for his hard work and we hung up.

2 Tim 2:15 (KJV): "Study to shew thyself approved unto God, a workman that needeth not to be ashamed, rightly dividing the word of truth."

I was definitely not what most would consider as 'religious'. I would say I was in relationship with the Father, Son and the Holy Spirit, which is why I go to him first, especially now having gone through this process. You know He knows me best, so why not go to the source directly. Learning how God thinks helps you see differently. It helps you see what's not visible with your natural eye.

As I hung up the phone said a quick prayer, God said, "I got this." So, I brushed off the disastrous news, picked up my bag and crutches, and headed to summer camp to continue the summer of discovering my God, my very best friend.

Jn 15:15 (NIV): "I no longer call you servants, because a servant does not know his master's business. Instead, I have called you friends, for everything that I learned from my Father I have made known to you."

11

I Am Who You Say I Am

Even though the doctors said I may have to relearn how to walk, playing basketball was still not even an option. They had to cut all the nerves and muscles in my leg, so the likelihood that all my feelings coming back enough to play sports was slim to none. Plus, my bone had been exposed to air so that's a whole different kind of pain. The doctor continued on to say that I would not be able to have children. But I pushed all that "worst case scenario" stuff to the side and just focused on making it through one day at a time.

First things first, walking. My leg just hung there while the physical therapist looked at me down the length of the poles. I was thinking to myself, "Yes, what do you want me to do?" My mind remembered how to walk, but my leg had amnesia.

We did some simple exercises at first and I really had to play a mental trick on myself so that I would not tense up and give into the fear that it may hurt or I may fall.

I had a great team of helpers at the physical therapy office. My mom paid extra to make sure I spent no time thinking about it, but moving and literally taking steps towards my recovery. That woman was relentless. She would not let me be too hard or soft on myself. I had some bouts of anger and fear, but as soon as I took a deep breath and closed my eyes, I saw Jesus standing there, arms opened wide saying, *"Come on, you can do it; I got this and I got you."*

What should have taken a year took literally months. I was beginning to be able to pick my foot up and even take steps with no crutches in six months! I was walking, and soon after that, I picked up my trusty friend, el basketball. The sound of the ball hitting the floor was music to my ears. I loved everything about basketball: the game, the science of it, and most of all, the language between you, the ball, and that hoop. I'll never forget when I launched my first shot and the ball trundled through the net…Swish! Nothing but net.

The following school year, I was back on the court, cheering on my teammates and wearing my uniform again. Only this year, I was at the number one school in Maui and playing varsity.

The drills were harder and the game was tougher, but the rewards for me were unimaginable. To everyone else, I was just another basketball player. But to God, I was more than a conqueror.

Rom 8:37: "Yet in all these things we are more than conquerors through Him who loved us"

For the rest of the time I was in school, I chose to give God my very best. Studying hard, reading my Word, not going out partying, but really focused on figuring out who I was in God. I didn't get a lot of playing time the first year, but definitely more the second. No one except God, my mom, and I knew how much pain I was in every time I put pressure on that leg or tried to go up for a layup. But I knew God had me. He was healer, my redeemer. my everything.

12

My Senior Year

I was doing great in school. Growing in my Word, actively sharing my testimony with anyone and everyone. I really felt like I had overcome so much that nothing could shake me now. I had a job, some friends, and I thought for once, after multiple absences, my Dad was back in my life for good. I was working on my Associate's degree and high school diploma at the same time, determined to be a good fit for any school that I might apply for. My mom even convinced me to go to the prom, which turned out to be so much fun. I took not one, but four girls from work. It was a blast. I was in the home stretch. My coach said scouts were coming to check us out and to make sure we were focused and playing our hearts out.

My mom was busy making plans for my birthday and upcoming graduation. She invited all my grandparents and friends to attend this massive celebration she had cooked up.

I remember coming home from school one day and saw two letters from colleges I applied to sitting on the counter. Wow, two in one week! I was so excited to see if I got in. I ripped through the first one. It said, "You have been accepted…" and so I tore open the next one, and again. "You have been accepted…!" What?? No way! I was thrilled.

I decided to wait till after dinner when both my parents were home to share my exciting news. I was getting anxious as my mom made dinner, but my dad did not come home till way after 8 pm. I was half asleep when he came in. He stalked over to me and said, "Junior, get up. I need to talk to you." He then went and woke my mother up as well and we met in the living room. I remember her and I looking at each other quite confused. He begins pacing back and forth. My mom says softly, "So, what's going on? She had that tone. That tone of disappointment and dread from times before when he announced he got laid off or gambled the rent money away.

He cleared his throat and said, "Well, I made a decision to move back to California. A truck is coming in the morning to pick up all my belongings, but don't worry, I will come back for your graduation day.

What the hell??, I said out loud, looking at the pool of tears running down my mother's face. He's doing it to us again. He's left so many times before; I don't even know why this surprised me, but it did. I shouted at him, *"Why? Why now? Why can't you wait three more weeks until I graduated? What's so important this time!* I got up, took the acceptance letters from behind my back and threw at him, "Here, I got into *both* schools, not that you care! I stormed out of the room crying because I didn't want him to see he hurt me. I prayed on my bed and wept, "God, you seeing this? How many times, God, how many times? All I want is a father who loves me, cares about me and is a good man and husband to my mom." And in that moment, I stopped, "Oh God, my mom." Darn it, I can't fix this for her either. God, what's wrong with us? Why is it so hard for him to love us? God talk to me before I really lose it. I am getting so angry, I've worked so hard, I've never gotten into any trouble, never done drugs, nothing!!! Why?!! God whispered in my ear, "This is not your fault. This is not your problem, it's mine. Trust me, I got this." A soft kind of wind blew over me and a peace and calm came over my emotions. Something I can't explain just flooded over me.

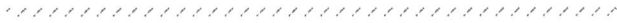

Phi 4:6-7: "Do not be anxious about anything, but in every situation, by prayer and petition, with thanksgiving, present your requests to God. And the peace of God, which transcends all understanding, will guard your hearts and your minds in Christ Jesus.

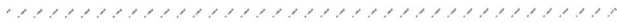

And:

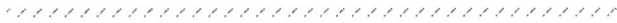

Jn 14:27: "Peace I leave with you; my peace I give you. I do not give to you as the world gives. Do

not let your hearts be troubled and do not be afraid."

I had a tournament the next week so I just focused on that. My mom was up worshipping every morning and night. She had peace, too. We just kept on moving forward, not really understanding, but yet, we did. Three weeks later, I graduated with honors. My parents and my grandparents were there. I chose to make my day as happy as possible so I just decided to be nice to my dad and honor him. God had taught me how to honor the position rather than the person. Honor him not because he expected it or earned it. For this pleased God.

Two days later, after my birthday party, I had to say goodbye to everyone on Maui that had become like family to me and head back to California with my mother. I looked at her as we sat on the plane and she just smiled and said, "Yes, God's got this, too."

God's love really does heal your heart and your mind in a way anger, bitterness or even revenge can't. But there was still something inside me that desired my father's love and approval no matter how much I tried to give it all to God.

13

God's Ways Are Not Our Ways

So here we are, me and my mother trying to settle in another new town. I had responded to the school of my choice, only to get a call from admissions saying that since we moved from Hawaii before the year started, I now had to pay out-of-state fees and I would be red-flagged from basketball because I already had my Associate's degree. *"What?! Okay, God, now I am being penalized for getting good grades and a degree? I've had it!"* Again, I prayed, frustrated that my life was always going to be a flippin' rollercoaster that I had no control of. So, I turned to my rock, my Word.

Is 55:8: "For my thoughts are not your thoughts, neither are your ways my ways," declares the Lord"

Okay God, what does that mean? Crickets... So, I stayed in my word for three days and fasted. I had done this with my mom before when she was seeking wisdom. It helps you hear clearly and not just let your emotions guide you.

Is 58:6: "Is not this the kind of fasting I have chosen: to loose the chains of injustice and untie the cords of the yoke, to set the oppressed free and break every yoke?"

On the third day, I got a call from a friend of mine that I knew from Youth With A Mission (YWAM). He asked me if I had any plans for the summer? I said, "No." He asked if I would be willing to come to Southern California to play in some overseas team's tournaments and at halftime give my testimony. "Are you kidding me? God *and* basketball? Yes, sir I'm in! I spoke to my mom and she said, Go, it's your time. So I did.

What an amazing time I had traveling to different high schools and stadiums, first in So-Cal, then in other states, and then in Northern Cal. I loved balling harder than ever, but more importantly, I loved sharing my God story. God had his hand on me every step of the way. I got invited to more camps and more tournaments. My life was coming into focus. And that's when I realized I didn't have to play college ball to make it to the NBA. Maybe I could just go straight to the NBA. One night as I laid my head down after a playing in a tournament, I said, "God, I know you are not a man that you should lie. You say "you got this," so I will leave it up to you. Use me to share my story to help others and give You glory.

Over the next few months, I visited sick kids in hospitals and brought hope, smiles and Jesus to them all. I helped several organizations start homeless ministries and even helped start a Kings Chapel for Dr Marocco in Northern California. A lot of times, we have heard God in regards to our purpose and our destiny, but in our excitement, we start to assume exactly how it was going to go. We focus on how others have done it and then think that's the way it's going to happen for us. But with God, it may not be so. His ways are not always are ways so we have to learn to ask God how He wants it done rather than making our own plans with our very, very limited knowledge. All I knew was God called and I said, "Yes." I really didn't understand my call per say, but I just knew I loved God and if He needed my life, He could have it.

After summer was over, I was asked to come play ball for not one team, but several teams. I attended tryouts and was given offers. I always came to practice earlier than anyone else and tried to be a leader on and off the courts, but my heart was always for Him. But I still had this one ache in my heart--I guess you could say it was an inner vow. I thought for sure if I made it this far, my dad would finally want to be in my life, that this would somehow prove to him that I was good enough to love. But instead, it brought out more resentment and competition on his part. He would only come around me now if he needed money. I believed God's Word and he knew it, throwing scriptures at me about honoring my parents or turning the other cheek. He would always come in and out of my life professing God had changed him, and I would let him back in only to be used and discarded again and again. So I filled every void in my life with basketball and other outreach events. I never got into drugs, alcohol or porn. But instead, I would go to several churches on Sunday and Wednesday and pray and worship. God was my father, my best friend and my refuge. Church was like going home after a long trip, or like going to see your grandparents. I felt safe and I knew my place there. Don't get me wrong, my mom always did her best to be there for me as best she could, but I was craving a fatherly bond from a man, a father that I could learn from. I wanted to belong. My grandfathers and great-grandfathers were getting older and some didn't even know God so those relationships were not that strong type of bond. I tried to put that on my coaches, but even though they were great coaches at basketball they were not good at life stuff. Same with my friends. They were great at talking about basketball and money, but not the rest. I found myself counseling them more than the other way around.

Then one day, I decided to cry out to God about this. I felt so alone on this journey and wanted God to come and fill this void for me once and for all. I knew that I wanted more, but what was it that God wanted for me right now? I felt like before I could leap into being a husband or a father, I needed to be "fixed" because my heart was (what I thought at the time was) broken. But really, God was there all along. He was expanding my heart to make room for my own family and wife. But the enemy knows the desires of your heart as well and that's why it is so important to know who you are and your worth for yourself. How? As the Word says,

Rom 15:4: "For everything that was written in the past was written to teach us, so that through the endurance taught in the Scriptures and the encouragement they provide we might have hope."

And:

2 Tim 2:15: "Study to shew thyself approved unto God, a workman that needeth not to be ashamed, rightly dividing the word of truth."

You know the saying, *hurt people hurt people.* Well, that's true. If you feel broken, you will attract brokenness. So instead of getting healed, even though I thought I was, I started trying to make my own family. I decided to move to San Diego, plug into church, and begin looking for my "wife". But that doesn't line up with God's will. His word says, "He who finds a wife finds a good thing." He who finds, not he who waits for God to bring him a wife. So, I thought it was my job to " find a "girl" and *make her* a wife. And I did.

Jam 1:4: "But let patience have its perfect work, that you may be perfect and complete, lacking nothing."

14

I Do

Ps 42:7: "Deep calls to deep in the roar of your waterfalls; all your waves and breakers have swept over me"

If you are operating out of lack or pain, you will draw that to yourself as well. I had gone out with a few girls from church, but all they wanted to do was party. They weren't looking to settle down. Well, I'm not that guy. I am not the party guy so those relationships ended just as quickly as they started. I began to talk to God about the courting process as I continued to go to church and began working a lot. It wasn't that I didn't trust God, I just felt like I knew what I wanted. *I got this.* I don't need to bug God about this. Wrong!

A few weeks later, I was at church and my pastor gave me a word about meeting my wife soon. I was like, *Oh, heck yeah!* My bank accounts, my jobs, my home and my ride were in order so just go ahead and bring her Lord! But again, the enemy will bring the counterfeit if you don't consult the Lord.

What is a counterfeit you ask? A counterfeit is something that is made in exact imitation of something valuable or important with the intention to deceive or defraud. Read that again. *Something made in exact imitation of something valuable with the intent to deceive or defraud.* The enemy is a master counterfeiter. He won't send one of his cronies after you with big horns and dressed in black. He'll send them looking and acting exactly how the gift God has for you looks and acts. You do not have enough knowledge to know this beforehand, only God does. He knows the end from the beginning. But let's say you have accepted your calling, you have given your life to God, and you have gone through the fire. Someone brand new in the faith with no experience, no wisdom and no understanding of this will get snared by the enemy because they aren't seasoned enough yet in spiritual warfare. Feelings of frustration, discouragement and maybe unworthiness will come in like a flood to discourage from continuing on with their calling. A tactic of the enemy is to get you attached to someone who is unequally yoked, which means not in agreement with your purpose and destiny. At this time, I thought as long as they are saved,

I'm all good. Wrong! I never inquired of the Lord to see who He had for me. Someone that would be aligned with His purpose and plan for my life.

One night, I was working security at my friend's bar in San Diego when a young woman walked in and started to ask me questions. We began talking. She wasn't drinking or dancing; she was just sitting there talking to me. We started talking about God, church, her son and how he loved basketball. At the time, she seemed very together, mature and stable, so I invited her to church the next day and she said, "Yes." *I thought* this was a clear sign from God so I took her to church, then to lunch. It went so well, she let me meet her son. He was a good kid, shy, and he was a good little ball player. He reminded me of myself. We started courting and married months later. I started coaching her son in basketball and everything seemed to be falling right into place. I got a coaching job and a young adult's pastoral position at a new church and thought everything was on track.

Months later, many, many, many trials came into play. The most outlandish one was my father showed back up. He took me and my new family to dinner not to tell me he was proud of what I was making of myself, but to tell me he was leaving the state, oh, and that basically he didn't want a relationship with me. It was time to "move on" as he put it. Then he needed to speak ill of my mom who recently had another battle with cancer and a stroke, saying, "She's not your problem; just let her go on with the Lord!

Needless to say, every childhood memory flood back in and wounded me all over again. My wife tried her best to make light of it, for my sake, but it seemed like she was mocking me, siding with him and condoning his views of me.

First wall went up.

Then more stress with money came into the picture. She was upset that I worked so much, yet, she was the one telling me to make more money and do less free stuff like ministry.

Second wall went up.

Next thing I know, I'm in a meeting with the pastor and he's saying I need to step down from ministry because *my wife is not ready for all this.* What?! News to me, talk about blind-sided.

Third wall went up.

In the blink of an eye, I was no longer preaching, trying to run two companies, and still coaching basketball. I've taken a few lumps, but I'm still standing. Then the enemy went in for the knockout. Mom takes a turn for the worse. Dang it! But my wife says, "Bring her here. I don't want you gone all the time taking care of her, bring her to our house for now."

Whew!, I thought. Okay, great, she's making an effort, so we move my mother in. Things are going great until the mother-in-law honeymoon period ended. The next thing I know, my wife's accusing me of not making her a priority, and cheating because I'm gone so much. Wait What??! In my mind, I'm doing all this for her, for our family, and our future. I had shared my dreams of what God had showed me. I even welcomed her input and encouraged her to be involved. She came to work with me numerous times and saw what I was doing. And of all things to accuse me of, *cheating*??! She knew how much I had to forgive my father for cheating on my mom, and how much I had *prayed for her* and a family. That truly showed me that she never knew me. She wounded me with her words and I had had it, I checked out! I was done trying to please people! I felt attacked from every side.

I had already sacrificed so much of myself, my vision, and my ministry to make her feel a part of it. And for her to attack my character, not just to my face, but also behind my back to others, I went into self-protection mode. Instead of going to God directly, I just went internal. At the time, I thought that was the same thing. But in hindsight I realized I just became a shell. I worked a ridiculous number of hours weekly and barely rested, not wanting to come home to bitterness and strife. That left me drained. My health started to take a turn for the worse just as my mom was starting to get better. She was well enough to move her into her own place thinking this would make things better at home. It didn't. First, I got the news that the bone cancer had returned and my business partner was wanting to dissolve our company *for personal reasons*. This was just too much for me to handle at one time. I crashed, hard. I literally shut down mentally, emotionally, and now, physically. All that remained of me was a shell.

"God, what's wrong with me? Why can't I catch a break?

I turned to a pastor friend for advice, but you know the saying, "Don't seek council from those who haven't been where you're going." So, I started watching a lot of T.D. Jakes. He was my surrogate mentor for me because he was a man with great vision, purpose, and spoke a lot on destiny. His book, *He-Motions*, and a few others became my new go-to. I was putting all my efforts into my remaining business and my word. I was so to myself; I didn't even share with my wife I was sick! At this point, I felt all I could do was damage control. Our relationship was already rocky and I thought I could leave her alone and God would speak to her. Wrong again.

Instead of God, she began taking counsel from her family and worldly counselors and friends who had never been married. She was wanting to go party, go on vacations, and basically get back to a material world. The last straw was her son's father started harassing us and accusing me of all kinds of ridiculous things because she was not allowing him to see their son. Somehow, I ended up in court. I've never been to court in my life, but here I am, having to defend myself against false accusations. Well, thank God, literally. When God says he will be your defender, He will. The judge laughed as he proceeded to drop all charges and that was that. I got to get myself together! I got to get back on track. Now I'm focused again on my health and putting some balance back in my life. I started going to the gym hard, eating right, and taking back control of my life.

Trying to reconcile and make the most of my marriage, I had asked my wife if she wanted to go to the gym with me. Sometimes she would, sometimes she wouldn't. We weren't better, but civil. I just needed peace and rest in my life and was trying to get it any way I could. So, after a long hard day at work, I decided to just go to the gym on the way home and get a quick one in and release some stress. Well, wouldn't you know, my wife shows up. "Why didn't you call me to come?" I apologized. I was just so beat trying to do a quick set. She stormed out. I finished my workout, and then went to sit in the sauna to keep myself calm. As I'm getting dressed, I got a text, "Don't bother coming home."

Here's where having a father would have been helpful. He probably would've told me to go home and talk it out with my wife. But no, that's not what I did. I just shook my head, called a buddy, and crashed on his couch. The next day, I went to home. The locks had been changed! And she filed a *TRO* - temporary restraining order-- so that I could come and retrieve my things *on a given date*! I was done, completely done this time. I was done convincing people to love me, done being a whipping post, done compromising my walk with God to please a woman who could love me or leave me that easy! D.O.N.E.! As the police officer served me the tro, I went to my car and just let out a scream, Ugh! God Why?? I have never been in trouble with the law, never put a hand to anyone. All I do is work hard and love others. Why is all this happening? God just whispered, "Son, give all this to me. Please son, trust me, I got this. I got you.

//

Mt 11:28-30: "Come to me, all you who are weary and burdened, and I will give you rest. Take my yoke upon you and learn from me, for I am gentle and humble in heart, and you will find rest for your souls. For my yoke is easy and my burden is light."

15

God Really Does Supply All Your Needs

Here I am, 32, and getting divorced, something I believed so strongly against.

God, whom am I? What do you want me to do?

I moved into a guestroom at a buddy's, me and my dog, Coco. I was battling depression, cancer, and an identity crisis all at once. I knew God had called me to ministry and to build his kingdom and to help the community. I also knew I wanted to be a husband and a father. I felt like a failure, but I didn't know why. I knew I had not cheated. It never even crossed my mind, but I also didn't make her happy. I was studying my word day and night and work the one business while phasing out the other. But what I should've been doing was trying to rest.

But I started to get into bodybuilding. I started meeting a lot of men and women who had overcome a lot of health crises and other life events with the help of fitness and bodybuilding. So, I thought, maybe this would help me feel more powerful, more determined, to give me answers and gain perspective on my body and my health. At this time, I was also celebrating my mom getting married to an incredible man named Eric. They met about eight years earlier, but he wasn't ready for the power- house woman my mom was, but he was a good guy. He came to some of my basketball games back then and supported me, coached me in a couple of tournaments, and prayed for me when I hurt no shoes to play in. This dude shows up with not one, not two, but three pairs of new shoes. He had played basketball all through college, but caught the entertainment bug after going to grad school. He was great at reading me and my game and giving me insight. But I was really super-excited for my mom because *he chose* to give up his Hollywood life and dreams to be a man after God's own heart and to be her husband to do with ministry with. Something my real father refused to do.

This was an answer to prayer for me as much as for her. Her health and well-being had fallen onto my shoulders when my biological father up and left her while she had been in a medically-induced coma after dying during surgery. He basically never would take care of her when she was sick, and she, by this time, had overcome cancer *nine times* and two strokes. My mom never complained. She always got right back up and went back to work, back to church, and taking care of me. So, of course, it was a no brainer that I would do the same for her. A burden others would say that was not mine to carry, but I say that's ridiculous. A) she's not a burden, and B), we are family. I watched my mom take care of her grandma with cancer, my paternal grandfather when he had bone marrow cancer, and numerous others. So why wouldn't I help her? She was my hero, my pastor, and my only parent. Her well-being was my responsibility

But now in walks Eric. He not only marries her and puts a smile on her face, he tells me, "J, you've done a great job helping mom, but she's my responsibility now. It's both my privilege and honor to protect her, care for her, and be with her. Wow, it had been seven years! Seven years since mom was able to care for herself or work. This was seriously such a gift for both of us. God is faithful and He knows our heart's desires and He wants to give us good gifts.

Lk 11:13: "If you then, though you are evil, know how to give good gifts to your children, how much more will your Father in heaven give the Holy Spirit to those who ask him!"

Well, with mom on her way to a new life, I started looking at my own. My divorce was about to be final so I decided to reach out one last time to my wife to see if this is really what she wants. I didn't have a peace so I needed to make sure. I prayed about it and the next day, I got invited to a friend's church... and there she was. So, I asked her if I could speak to her? We stepped outside and it is there she let me know that "God has big things for you and it's just too much for me. I'm not the right one for you." Wow, well ok then. I blessed her and kept it moving.

With that relationship basically finished, I started going to the gym two or three times a day. It became my second home. I was really trying to beat this cancer and turning excruciatingly bad pain into good pain that I controlled. Lifting weights really helped me change my mindset. During one of my workouts, I met a girl there whose father and I had been friends for years. He's a great pastor, so I thought, *Well, maybe this one is the one?*

But again, everything looked great. She was great. We went to church. We worked out together. We liked hanging out with each other. Great! And then I found myself watering my walk down and dumbing myself down to fit into her world instead of God's.

After 10 grueling months. Eric came to me and said, J, you need to know who you are to God. Yes, you are humble, and yes you live for God, but do you really know what He thinks of you? Nobody ever said that to me before, and he quickly began to tell me who I was in God. Now I'm sure my mom had told me some of this before, but to me, that was just mom talking. But this was a man, a mighty man of God, who was generously pouring into me without me ever asking him to. He counseled me to stop trying to find a wife, but to let God show me who He's chosen *just for me*. One He feels is worthy of me. Wow, this was something I had never heard before. He went on to tell me things his father shared with him about God and about life, and I started to see myself as a man, no longer a boy or a servant of God, but a man, a man of God. A King. A Lion.

Eric began to show me I had a lot of the same qualities as leaders and men in the bible, born not because of money, or status, or even because of a wife or kids, but because *of my heart.* He explained to me that few men have a heart as pure as mine. He began to explain why my biological father had a hard time relating to me, not because I wasn't loveable. But because of The Glory I carried inside of me. He began to explain why women might seem to be attracted to me, but really it was just to the anointing. If they pretend to be Christians, God's testing would prove otherwise, because only God really knows a person's heart and motives. Whoa, life was really starting to shift for me.

In the midst of the turmoil in my new relationship, I began to have health issues. I became extremely dehydrated, which caused me to have seizures. As the stress and strain of life intensified, I suffered a mild heart attack and stroke. And who was there at the hospital every single time, who took me to every appointment, who prayed over me, read the Word to me, and basically cared for me during my recovery, Eric.

My heart was so full and overflowing even though my body was trying to shut down. Eric was right there with my mom every step of the way. One day, as Eric was picking me up from the ground after a seizure, he looked me in my eyes and said, "Come on, J, you're good. God's got this!

16

Adoption

Rom 8:15: "The Spirit you received does not make you slaves, so that you live in fear again; rather, the Spirit you received brought about your adoption to sonship. And by him we cry, "Abba, Father."

I had just got the papers that stated my divorce was final. I have no more business and I'm living with my mom and Eric. Due to the seizures, I had not been able to drive. Between the heart attack, the stroke and seizures, there's been a lot of trauma to my body, including swelling on my brain. But I am hopeful, but feeling frustrated I'm about to turn 33 and my parents are still taking care of me. I'm too old for this. God had always spoke to me about my 33rd birthday being *life changing*. Trying to stay positive and upbeat, I started to focus on my walk with God again, hanging out with my parents, and connecting with basketball by coaching young kids. I started to see light at the end of the tunnel.

One Sunday, we all went to church as a family and Rex Crain, a powerful man of God, was speaking that day. He called me down to the altar and gave me a prophetic word that the enemy has fought hard to keep you from your calling, but God chose you, and God will see *His prophesy* fulfilled *in you*! Time for your ministry and life to go next level.

Yes!, that sounds great! Thank you, God!

The following week, my parents bought tickets to a business event called Life On Fire. We were going to go next level in business and ministry by coaching, but I had no idea what I was really instore for. It was a three-day event where we talked about every part of life except business. Instead, it talked about how everything you have done and will do is part of building your legacy. After the first night, Eric and my mom sat me down at the kitchen table and Eric began to share his heart about inheritance. About how God grafts us into His family and how God does not just save us, but He chooses us and adopts us so that we become heirs with Him.

Rom 8:17: "Now if we are children, then we are heirs—heirs of God and co-heirs with Christ, if indeed we share in his sufferings in order that we may also share in his glory."

I look at my mom and she's got tears in her eyes. I am so used to bad news. Bad reports and family meetings equal bad news for me. But as I was watching her face and listening to Eric, I started to imagine what horrible thing is about to happen? Had I been here to long? Is Eric and my mom splitting up? Do they want me to leave?! What already! Just tell me!

The next words that came out of Eric's mouth seemed like they came out in slow motion. "I. Want. To. Adopt. You." Wait, what did he just say? I sat stunned, tears running down my face and Eric's. I said, "I'm sorry, what was the last part? I think I missed something?" Eric said, "You know your father chose to leave your life, but God has given me a love for you as if you were always mine. Can I adopt you?"

I sat there stunned replaying the entire message. The words *adopt you* rang in my head over and over. I said, "Yes, sure, I would like that." He then took the adoption papers from my mom and said, "You choose, I can adopt you spiritually, legally but I also can give you a whole new name, my name. What do you think?!" I could not believe my ears. God is so into the details. Here I am about to be 33 in a few weeks *and* I'm being adopted, too! I asked if I could have some time to think about it all. They said, "Yes," and I went to my room, closed the door, and fell to my knees and wept.

"God, is this you? Is this the answer to my prayers since I was a little boy?"

I tried calling and texting my biological father, who I had not talked to for almost two years now, and the number was disconnected. So, I knew, ok God this is real. How do you want me to do this? Then God showed me others in the bible whom he gave a new name to.

Gen 17:3-6: "Abram fell facedown, and God said to him, "As for me, this is my covenant with you: You will be the father of many nations. No longer will you be called Abram; your name will be Abraham, for I have made you a father of many nations. I will make you very fruitful; I will make nations of you, and kings will come from you."

Then He said to me, "Your biological father has done all he could. He chose his path. It's ok to choose yours and *what I have for you is for you.*" So the next morning, we went back for day two of the event. I handed Eric the signed papers and said, I would be honored to be your son and to have a new name. We hugged and left for the event. The next four days was a whirlwind. We filed the papers, celebrated my 33rd birthday, I got some clarity on what my new goals were in my life, and I got healed from a lot of what I thought were failures. Now I know they were nothing more than tests, tests that I passed with flying colors. God closed doors and removed all those who would not be able to support me or go with me into my destiny and calling.

One week later, I officially became Eric's son and got my brand-new name and birth certificate. I was able to bless my biological father, release him to God, and move forward into my new beginnings.

17

If I Write It, It Comes To Pass

One of the best things of my life has been my mother teaching me the power of a vision how to write down and make it plain

Hab 2:2: "Write down the revelation and make it plain on tablets so that a herald may run with it."

Well, at that three-day event, with the help of my team mates, I discovered who I am at my core:

I am a healthy, wealthy, lovable husband!

I wore this on a giant poster for a whole day and yelled it out loud whenever I was prompted. As we were wrapping up from the event, they told us to write a letter about our future career, business whatever we wanted to see come to past in the next six months. My group partner pastor suggested I write the letter about my future wife and family and the life I was believing for in a partner, best friend, and a soul mate. So, I did just that. I spent a few hours on it. I poured my heart and soul into, not leaving out any details, and then I read it out loud to my group. They all asked me more about her like her name and how long have you dated? But the truth was it was all coming from my heart and visions God gave me.

I had never met her yet in real life. Or so I
thought.

Over the course of the next few weeks, I
started having visions of this one friend of mine.
She lived in another state and had two boys, one
of which I mentored from time to time.
I spoke to her casually on the phone, but mostly
just to her oldest son. He had an estranged
relationship with his father and was being bullied
at school. I would talk to him and encourage him.

But after the one vision, I asked God, "Is this
who you are highlighting?" My dad had told me
before "God will highlight your wife to you." So,
I stood on that and just kept it in prayer. Next
thing I know, she's texting me, "Hey, I'm bring
my son to California for his birthday and he
would really like to meet you in person if you
have some free time." "Okay now God, you
know I am just going into remission, got a new

name, and haven't even started working, so is this really the timing?"

And of course, God says, *"I got this."*

So, I meet them and spend the day at Universal Studios with them. I'm giving them the deluxe tour of Los Angeles and all the tourist spots they see on Tv. Everything just flowed. Her and I had so much in common with health, fitness, overcoming trials and tribulations, our parents are in ministry. Like all the boxes were being checked off. So, we sit down for dinner on her last night in town and we just start talking about the future. She asks me if she can share a story with me? I said, "Sure." Next thing I know, she's telling me how she hired a life coach and the coach kept asking her what do you want for with your life? And she started telling me how she wanted to be married and have a full-time father for her sons... *and to do ministry.* She goes on to tell me how her coach encouraged her to wrote a letter. Okay, wait, stop right there. Did she just say a letter?!

Okay God, I'm listening. I tell her to go on. She says, "So I wrote God a letter about wanting to let go of the pain of my past failed marriage, my 'tough girl-I don't need a man' attitude, and most of all, to give my life and my future back to Him so I can fulfill my legacy in ministry. "Okay, girl, you betta stop! is what I said in my head, but I kept quiet and smiled as she continued speaking for the next 20 minutes. I looked up at one point to the heavens, and I heard got say, *"Didn't I tell you, I got this!*

Two months later, I married that woman. Her name is Veronica. She moved to California with her/our boys and we are building our ministry business and life together. Today, my father, Eric, and I have a ministry for young men and boys called the Lionz Den where we mentor, encourage, and teach life lessons to boys and men alike who have daddy issues. We give each one a father's blessing so they can become the kings they are called to be.

Thank you, God, you really do got this!

Love Letter To Jamez

Jamez, when I think of you, it reminds me of the love of God. You are someone very special person to me, when I see you, I see a warrior, a strong man, an overcomer, a chosen man of God. I remember the day we met at Sprouts in the summer of 2016. It was like love at first sight. We became friends first, but you're definitely someone I've always admired from afar. Yet, I always felt you very close to me, especially in times of hardship as you were always there to intercede for me. You walked me through the saddest & darkest moments in my life for two consecutive years. You inspired me to want to seek and experience God & His Grace in a way that only someone who's walked through and gone through the things you have could. Getting closer to God again and writing that letter of declaration in April 2019 changed my life. I surrendered my will to the Lord and asked for the desires of my heart. I didn't know that was only the beginning of a lifetime. My greatest adventure awaits ahead of me. I asked God for true love, peace, joy and happiness. These are the things I had in my heart and mind even after my first failed attempt in marriage, I was hurt and broken, but as usual, God had a greater plan for me. And little did I know that not only were you included in God's plan all along, but you've also dreamt of having a wife that you've prayed for since childhood. I thank heaven for bringing us together despite all the obstacles that the enemy attempted to throw our way. The multiple challenges we had to go through to make it to the altar, that only proved we were both committed to pursue our dreams together. God is the God of details and you are everything I prayed for in a man since childhood, as well and so much more. From waking up every morning speak words of affirmation over my life, praying blessings over me, intimacy with you, seeking God together, and achieving life goals, to cooking the best meals and treating me like a true Queen daily. You are an amazing stepfather to our boys, Jomar and Javian. You have created a safe home for us and we are proud to be part of your life. I'm honored to be your wife, your best friend, your lioness. It is an honor to watch you grow and become the man God has called you to be. I am so blessed to have you in my life and I wanted to write this letter to say thank you, on behalf of myself, our boys and thousands of lives you've impacted throughout your journey. The best is yet to come!

Baby:

You are Loved

You are Chosen

You are Honored

You are Respected

You are Valued

You are Cared For

You are a Loving Husband

You are an Amazing Stepfather

You are the Head and not the tale

You are Above and not beneath

You are a Warrior

You are an Overcomer

You are a Lion

With Love,

Your Wife & Best Friend,

Veronica Ingram

Jamez Ingram

About The Author...

Jamez Ingram is a tour-de-force! He knowz what it means to be all in with God. Hiz full trust in The Almighty. He haz had a personal relationship with Jesus from birth and hiz extremely generous and joyous heart makez him an absolute threat to satan and his kingdom. Despite many obstaclez in life: an absent father, school bullying, cancer at ages 14 and 20, suffered a stroke, two heart attackz, and coded twice, he haz taken life's sourest lemonz and made the sweetest lemonade.

Hiz passion in life is to inspire and transform the underdog, the outcast, the downtrodden, and the fatherless into the precious gemz God created them to be. Not only haz he mastered the art of forgiveness, he's a living billboard of it.

From feeding the homeless, coaching youth basketball, and training elite fitness athletes to instilling his God-given wisdom of health, nutrition, and uplifting encouragement to God's children of all walks of life, Jamez has inspired, healed, empowered, and transformed thousandz of otherz for the kingdom of God.

Because of Jamez' mountain-moving faith, he not only trusts God for the impossible for himself, he believez it for others, too! Hiz destiny is to create a global health revolution and effect true and permanent change in the lives of others.

Jamez Ingram